Published simultaneously in 1995 by Exley Publications in Great Britain, and Exley Giftbooks in the USA.

12 11 10 9 8 7

ISBN 1-85015-643-3

Edited and pictures selected by Helen Exley.
Pictures researched by Image Select International.
Typesetting by Delta, Watford.
Printed in China.

Exley Publications Ltd, 16 Chalk Hill, Watford, Herts WDI 4BN, United Kingdom.
Exley Publications LLC, 232 Madison Avenue, Suite 1206, New York, NY 10016, USA.

Acknowledgements: The publishers are grateful for permission to reproduce copyright material. While every effort has been made to trace copyright holders, the publishers would be pleased to hear from any not here acknowledged.
Bill Cosby: extracts from "Fatherhood" © 1986 by William H. Cosby Jr. Used by permission of Doubleday, a division of Bantam Doubleday Dell Publishing Group Inc.; Joyce Grenfell: extract from "Joyce By Herself and Her Friends", published by Futura 1981 © Joyce Grenfell Memorial Trust 1980. Reprinted by permission of Little, Brown and Co.; Lee Iacocca: extract from "Talking Straight" with Sonny Kleinfeld © 1988 by Lee Iacocca. Reprinted by permission of Bantam, a division of Bantam Doubleday Dell Publishing Group Inc.; Laurie Lee: extracts from "The First Born" from "I Can't Stay Long". Reprinted by permission of Penguin Books Ltd.; Cyra McFadden: extract taken from The San Francisco Examiner, June 19, 1988 © The San Francisco Examiner; Stephen Spender: "To My Daughter" from "Collected Poems" 1928-1985 and "Selected Poems" by Stephen Spender, © 1955 by Stephen Spender. Reprinted by permission of Ed Victor Ltd.; Harry Stein: extract from "Esquire", October 1981 c 1981 by Harry Stein. Reprinted with permission of the author; Lawrence Weschler: extract from "The New Yorker", 9 March 1987 © 1987 by The New Yorker Magazine, Inc.
Picture Credits: Exley Publications is very grateful to the following individuals and organizations for permission to reproduce their pictures: Archiv Für Kunst (AKG), Art Resource (AR), The Bridgeman Art Library (BAL), Chris Beetles Gallery (CBG), Christie's Images (CI), Edimedia (EDM), Fine Art Photographic Library Ltd (FAP), Giraudon (GIR), Image Select (IS), Roger-Viollet (RV), Scala (SCA), Statens Konstmuseer (SKM).
Cover: Arthur Hughes "L'Enfant Perdu" (detail) (CI); title page: K. Grob (CI); page 6: © 1995 Antoni Vila Arrufat (1894-1989) "A Girl Reading", Art Museum, Barcelona (BAL); page 8: Frans Wiesenthal, Whitford & Hughes, London (BAL); page 10: © 1995 Mary Cassatt (1844-1926) "Girl in Garden", Musée d'Orsay, Paris (SCA); page 12: © 1995 Repine (1844-1930) "Portrait of L. M. Audreieur, Tret jakov Gallery, Moscow (EDM); page 15: Albert Neuhuys, Galerie George, London (BAL); page 16: Rfanov (EDM); page 19: August Muller, Bradford City Art Gallery & Museums (BAL); page 21: Porfini Krylov (SCA) ; page 23 : Arthur Hacker, Galerie George, London (BAL); page 25: Amelia Bauerle (CBG); page 26: François, Gerard, Louvre, Paris (BAL/GIR); page 28: Carl Larsson (SKM); page 30/31: Carl Spitzweg (AKG); page 32: © 1995 John Quincey Adams (1874-1932) "Her First Recital" (AKG); page 34: Jenny NystromStoopendal (SKM); page 37: 1995 Robort Medley "The Butcher's Shop", Private Collection (BAL); page 39 © 1995 Ilja Repin (1844-1930) "Portrait of a Girl", Tret jakov Gallery, Moscow (SCA); page 41: Giovanni Giacometti (AKG); page 42: T. Gaponenko (SCA); page 45: Serov Valentin (SCA); page 46: (c 1995 Bernard de Hoog (1866-1943) "A Father's Love" (CI); page 49: Cc 1995 Janet Fisher "Distant Thoughts" Whitford & Hughes, London (BAL); page 51: P. W. Keller-Reutlingen (AKG); page 53: George Elgar Hicks (EDM); page 54: Hartmut Genz (AKG); page 57: R. Bong (AKG); page 59: (AKG); page 61: Sir Lawrence Alma-Tadema (RV).

THE LOVE BETWEEN
Fathers and Daughters

A HELEN EXLEY GIFTBOOK

NEW YORK • WATFORD, UK

"I know I have my father wrapped around my finger, but he has me wrapped around his."

HOLLY HESTON,
DAUGHTER OF CHARLTON HESTON

"The most important relationship within the family, second only to that of husband and wife, is the relationship between father and daughter."

DAVID JEREMIAH

"She didn't love her father – she idolized him. He was the one great love in her life. No other man ever measured up to him."

MARY S. LOVELL,
ABOUT BERYL MARKHAM

"All dads have their special whistle, their special call. Their own knock. Their way of walking.
Their imprint on our lives.
We think we forget but then, out of the darkness, comes a little trill of notes and our hearts lift. And we are five years old again and waiting for Dad's footsteps on the gravel path."

PAM BROWN, b.1928

"With my father life became an adventure. The minute he walked in the door at night, even the house seemed to take on a new energy, like a surge of electricity. Everything became charged, brighter, more colorful, more exciting....
All fathers are, at first, heroes to their daughters, even when they're anything but heroic."

VICTORIA SECUNDA

"Every day of my life has been a gift from him. His lap had been my refuge from lightning and thunder. His arms had sheltered me from teen-age heartbreak. His wisdom and understanding had sustained me as an adult."

NELLIE PIKE RANDALL

"Having a child alters the rights of every man, and I don't expect to live as I did without her. I am hers to be with, and hope to be what she needs, and know of no reason why I should ever desert her."

LAURIE LEE, b.1914

"When you are a father, and you
hear your children's voices, you will
feel that those little ones are akin to
every drop in your veins; that they
are the very flower of your life and
you will cleave so closely to them
that you seem to feel every
movement that they make."

HONORÉ DE BALZAC (1799-1850),
FROM "LE PÈRE GORIOT"

"She climbed into my lap and curled into the crook of my left arm. I couldn't move that arm, but I could cradle Ashtin in it. I could kiss the top of her head. And I could have no doubt that this was one of the sweetest moments of my life."

DENNIS BYRD, ABOUT HIS DAUGHTER

"Her father was her friend and mentor, who taught her to read, love books, type, swim, and ride a bike. 'I spent hours with him in his study, going for walks, going to the church, helping him garden, sitting quietly while he wrote his sermons.'

It sounds like the perfect father/daughter relationship except for one worm in the apple. 'I think I was his favourite but I have never dared ask my sisters if they think so too, possibly because I'm afraid they'd both say that they were.'"

CYRA MCFADDEN ABOUT A VICAR'S DAUGHTER IN HAMPSHIRE, ENGLAND

"A friend of ours, suddenly
a father, writes:
Thirty minutes after her birth, my
daughter was already taking my
measure. She lay in my lap,
startlingly alert, scanning me as I
scanned her, our gazes moving about
each other's bodies, limbs, faces, eyes
– repeatedly returning to the eyes,
returning and then locking.... My
eyes locked on hers, I'd had a sense
that I was gazing into origins – that
this gaze of hers was welling up at
me from deep beyond the past's past.
Of course, that sense of things was
all wrong, for, eye to eye, it was *she*
who was gazing into the past. I was
gazing into the future's future."

LAWRENCE WESCHLER,
FROM "THE NEW YORKER", MARCH 9, 1987

"Then they handed her to me, stiff
and howling, and I held her for the
first time and kissed her, and she
went still and quiet as though
by instinctive guile, and I was
utterly enslaved by her flattery
of my powers."

LAURIE LEE, b.1914,
FROM "THE FIRSTBORN"

"He grows with her,

learning as they go. He

feels with her – each

restlessness, each fear, each

pain. She laughs and he is

overjoyed. She reaches out

her little arms to him and

he rejoices. She sleeps on

his shoulder and he

does not move, for fear of

waking her."

PAM BROWN, b.1928

"I love my little girl an extraordinary amount; I have, in fact, surprised myself with my talent for fathering. Since her birth I have been so wholly preoccupied with the minutiae of her progress – from the growth of the microscopic hairs on her bald head to the lengthening of her attention span – that I have been effectively lost to the larger world."

HARRY STEIN,
FROM "ESQUIRE", OCTOBER 1981

Bright clasp of her whole
hand around my finger,
My daughter, as we walk
together now.
All my life, I'll feel a ring
invisibly
Circle this bone with shining:
when she is grown
Far from today as her
eyes are far already.

STEPHEN SPENDER, b.1909

"Men who have daughters needn't seek power in the boardroom or the bedroom, on the playing field or on the battlefield. They already have enormous influence.

They are No. 1 in their daughters' lives, and not only on Father's Day.

Fathers are the first men women love. We long for their approval, and when it's withheld, may decide to go outside and eat worms."

CYRA MCFADDEN

"One word of command from me is obeyed by millions ... but I cannot get my three daughters, Pamela, Felicity and Joan, to come down to breakfast on time."

VISCOUNT ARCHIBALD WAVELL
(1883-1950)

"There have been many times when I thought other people might be better singers or better musicians or prettier than me, but then I would hear Daddy's voice telling me to never say never, and I would find a way to squeeze an extra inch or two out of what God had given me."

BARBARA MANDRELL

"I was not close to my father, but he was very special to me. Whenever I did something as a little girl – learn to swim or act in a school play, for instance – he was fabulous. There would be this certain look in his eyes. It made me feel great."

DIANE KEATON

"The most important thing about our time together was this: whatever his politics or view of the role of women, he never made me think there was anything I couldn't do."

SUSAN KENNEY

"Almost every time I watch my daughters playing near me, especially in a physical way, an unusual feeling takes hold of me. I do not identify with the big smiling male whose offspring play at his feet, although I do expect to feel like this, looking at their tiny bodies and my own big one. On the contrary, I feel small and open. I feel as if the three of us are learning independently how to be dependent on one another."

MORDECHAI RIMOR

"He feels with her – each restlessness, each fear, each pain. She laughs and he is overjoyed. She reaches out her little arms to him and he rejoices. She sleeps on his shoulder and he does not move, for fear of waking her. He shows her marvels and lives her astonishment in bird and cat and falling leaf. He asks for kisses. Hugs. The invisible gifts that she bestows on those she loves – held carefully between minute thumb and finger. He fields her as she falls. Wraps her against the cold. Dries her from her bath. Boasts casually to friends of her achievements. Hoards photographs in case he should forget.
All disappointments, all failures fade like mist before this golden girl.
His daughter."

PAM BROWN, b.1928

"It doesn't make any difference how much money a father earns, his name is always Dad-Can-I; and he always wonders whether these little people were born to beg. I bought each of my five children everything up to a Rainbow Brite jacuzzi and still I kept hearing 'Dad, can I get... Dad, can I go... Dad, can I buy...' ...Sometimes, at three or four in the morning, I open the door to one of the children's bedrooms and watch the light softly fall across their little faces. And then I quietly kneel beside one of the beds and just look at the girl lying there because she is so beautiful. And because she is not begging. Kneeling there, I listen reverently to the sound of her breathing.
And then she wakes up and says, 'Dad, can I...'"

BILL COSBY, b.1937, FROM "FATHERHOOD"

"The father of a daughter, especially one in her teens, will find that she doesn't like to be seen walking with him on the street. In fact, she will often ask him to walk a few paces behind. The father should not take this outdoor demotion personally; it is simply a matter of clothes. His are rotten. Every American daughter is an authority on fashion, and one of the things she knows is that her father dresses like somebody in the Mummers Parade."

BILL COSBY, b.1937, FROM "FATHERHOOD"

"No man can possibly know what life means, what the world means, what anything means, until he has a child and loves it. And then the whole universe changes and nothing will ever again seem exactly as it seemed before."

LAFCADIO HEARN (1850-1904)

"Arthur always had his arms around [his daughter] Camera. When he talked about her, his face would light up like stars in the sky. He showed more feeling for his daughter than I had seen him show his whole life."

HORACE ASHE,
UNCLE OF ARTHUR ASHE

"He loves his children not because everything in them is lovely and according to his liking, but because there is a real incomprehensible bond which is stronger than fiction."

LEROY BROWNLOW,
FROM "A FATHER'S WORLD"

"Once I picked up Lia at Brownie
camp. She was six years old and
came running out to the car in her
new khaki uniform with an orange
bandanna around her neck and a
little beanie on her head. She had just
made it into the Potawatami Tribe.
She had hoped to join the Nava-joes,
as she called them, but she was
turned down. Still she was
excited, and so was I.
Funny thing, I missed an important
meeting that day, but for the
life of me I have no recollection of
what it was."

LEE IACOCCA, b.1924,
FROM "TALKING STRAIGHT"

"As I start the twilight years of my
life, I try to look back and figure out
what it was all about. I'm still not
sure what is meant by good fortune
and success. I know fame and power
are for the birds. But then suddenly
life comes into focus for me. And, ah,
there stand my kids. I love them."

LEE IACOCCA, b.1924,
FROM "TALKING STRAIGHT"

"He is totally transformed by his first daughter. There is a gentleness about him that even love never discovered. He holds her like a flower, like thinnest glass. He wonders at this new and lovely life, incredible in its perfection."

PAM BROWN, b.1928

"You appear to me so superior, so elevated above other men, I contemplate you with such a strange mixture of humility, admiration, reverence, love, and pride, that very little superstition would be necessary to make me worship you as a superior being.... I had rather not live than not be the daughter of such a man."

THEODOSIA BURR,
IN A LETTER TO HER FATHER
AARON BURR

"With all my heart I wish all the loving fathers of this world – cut off from their families by want or work or war – could be safe home again. For I know how much it means to have such a father – how much I need him in the small, everyday things – and just how much he needs me."

PAM BROWN, b.1928

"The lead in the old man's feet and
hanging hands
Weighs in my heart and in my head.
Where is that laughing creature,
mountain high,
The dear companion of another day?

We walked together then, on
Saturdays
Went to the galleries and heard the
Proms,
Saw the play from the pit,
And argued and walked and talked
and walked and walked,
Father and daughter,
Liking the same poor puns,
Meeting on common ground.
His judgments all were true,
I had no doubts at all,
He knew.

**JOYCE GRENFELL (1910-1979),
FROM "FATHER AND DAUGHTER"**

" You will never be free again.
You live two lives now,
hers and your own.
And the greatest pain is having to let
her make her own choices –
whatever your experience foretells.
Mercifully, this life link carries
happiness as well as heartache. You
are allowed to touch her joys, to
share the triumphs and excitements.
Distance cannot divide you. There
will be nights without sleep. Days of
waiting for a word. But letters.
Unexpected phone calls. The
astonishment of her standing on the
doorstep when you thought her half
a world away. And happiness
beyond anything you ever thought
possible. Surprises. Amazement.
For she is your diamond daughter.
She can cut across your
heart and mind."

ROSANNE AMBROSE-BROWN, b.1943

"How pleasant it is for a father to sit at his child's table. It is like an aged man reclining under the shadow of an oak he had planted."
SIR WALTER SCOTT (1771-1832)

"Thirty-four years of unbroken kindness, of cloudless sunshine, of perpetual joy, of constant love. Thirty-four years of happy smiles, of loving looks and gentle words, of generous deeds. Thirty-four years, a flower, a palm, a star, a faultless child, a perfect woman, wife, and mother."

ROBERT G. INGERSOLL
(1833-1899), IN A BIRTHDAY
NOTE TO HIS DAUGHTER EVA

"My dad is the backbone of our family. Any problem that I've ever had, he's always been there for me."
WHITNEY HOUSTON

"My father is the standard by which all subsequent men in my life have been judged."
KATHRYN MCCARTHY GRAHAM

"I was my father's daughter.... He is dead now and I am a grown woman and still I am my father's daughter.... I am many things besides, but I am daddy's girl too and so I will remain – all the way to the old folks' home."
PAULA WEIDEGER